Cognitive Behavioral Therapy

Practical Tips on How to Conquer Psychological Disorders and Take Back Control of Your Life

Preface

This book, *"Cognitive Behavioral Therapy: Practical Tips on How to Conquer Psychological Disorders and Take Back Control of Your Life"*, is a self-help guide, intended for individuals who want to have their life back despite their psychological disorders.

If you're haunted by fear and anxiety, or feel depressed and hopeless, this book will provide you guidelines in taking hold of the steering wheel of your life.

CBT is so broad, encompassing other vital disciplines, so the chapters focus more on the topics that would change your way of thinking to a more positive one.

There are no promises, because you – alone - can decide whether to fix the mess in your life or not. Nevertheless, if you religiously follow these self-help guidelines provided in this book, you can acquire the skills in overcoming your psychological problems.

Concrete examples are also given to provide you with an exact blueprint on what to do. With little or no active participation of a psychotherapist, you can certainly do well on your own.

Continue reading and learn the steps in coping with your condition.

©Copyright 2017 by R. Davis. All rights reserved.

This document is geared towards providing exact and reliable information in regards to the topic and issue covered. The publication is sold with the idea that the publisher is not required to render accounting, officially permitted, or otherwise, qualified services. If advice is necessary, legal or professional, a practiced individual in the profession should be ordered.

- From a Declaration of Principles which was accepted and approved equally by a Committee of the American Bar Association and a Committee of Publishers and Associations.

In no way is it legal to reproduce, duplicate, or transmit any part of this document in either electronic means or in printed format. Recording of this publication is strictly prohibited and any storage of this document is not allowed unless with written permission from the publisher. All rights reserved.

The information provided herein is stated to be truthful and consistent, in that any liability, in terms of inattention or otherwise, by any usage or abuse of any policies, processes, or directions contained within is the solitary and utter responsibility of the recipient reader. Under no circumstances will any legal responsibility or blame be held against the publisher for any reparation, damages, or monetary loss due to the information herein, either directly or indirectly.

Respective authors own all copyrights not held by the publisher.

The information herein is offered for informational purposes solely, and is universal as so. The presentation of the information is without contract or any type of guarantee assurance.

The trademarks that are used are without any consent, and the publication of the trademark is without permission or backing by the trademark owner. All trademarks and brands within this book are for clarifying purposes only and are the owned by the owners themselves, not affiliated with this document.

Cognitive Behavioral Therapy   1

Practical Tips on How to Conquer Psychological Disorders and Take Back Control of Your Life 1

Preface   2

Chapter 1: Introduction to Cognitive Behavioral Therapy 7

Chapter 2: History of Cognitive Behavioral Therapy   11

Chapter 3: Understanding the Power of the Mind   14

Chapter 4: Know Thyself, a Self-Assessment   21

Chapter 5: What You Think is What You Are   31

Chapter 6: Understanding Your Fear and Anxiety   35

Chapter 7: Setting Your Goals in Resolving Your Fears and Anxieties 46

Chapter 8: Implementing Your Goals for Fear and Anxiety Management   50

Chapter 9: Work Sheets for Fear and Anxiety Management   58

Chapter 10: Recording Your Thought Processes 60

Chapter 11: Evaluating Your Progress   63

Chapter 12: Understanding Your Anger and Depression   66

Chapter 13: Setting Your Goals to Cope with Anger and Depression   68

Chapter 14: Implementing Your Goals to Cope with Anger and Depression   70

Chapter 15: Recording Your Thought Processes 73

Chapter 16: Evaluating Your Progress   75

Chapter 17: Mindfulness and Self-Reflection in CBT   77

Chapter 18: Appraising Threats Accurately   81

Chapter 19: How You Can Take Back Control of Your Life   84

Chapter 20: Valuable Tips in Cognitive Behavioral Therapy 86

Conclusion   89

Chapter 1: Introduction to Cognitive Behavioral Therapy

So much have been said about Cognitive Behavioral Therapy (CBT) that some readers are confused as to what it really is. So, let's define the term in the simplest way possible.

What is Cognitive Behavioral Therapy?

CBT is a method of treatment for a number of psychological conditions using structured steps to change how the person thinks, and consequently, the way he acts and behaves. It can be coupled with other synergistic drugs and strategies.

Understandably, CBT does not work with all individuals. There is no single, perfect method that could cure all psychological ailments. It's still a case to case basis.

To explain CBT in the simplest form: CBT changes how the person feels by changing the way he thinks.

Pros and Cons of CBT

For you to know more about CBT; here are its pros and cons.

Pros

- It's a good alternative treatment for anxiety, some phobias, mental disorders, depression, fears and eating disorders.

- It's none invasive, so it's convenient.

- It doesn't have serious side-effects during and after treatment.

- The principles used in CBT can be used to develop your personality and optimism in life.

- Knowledge transfer is easy through various teaching modes, such as videos, texts, self-help eBooks and blogs.

- Treatment is shorter compared to other 'talking' therapies.

- It can be used in congruence with most medications.

- The tenets are practical and can be used in everyday life.

- It is goal-oriented; hence results would be more successful.

Cons

- You would have to participate more actively, with you doing most of the tasks (home works). It's you who truly changes yourself. The resources are only there to help you.

- It may not work with individuals who have severe mental conditions.

- You may feel uncomfortable, at times, because you're confronting your emotions.

- You may find the homework time-consuming.

- It will not focus on the underlying cause of other unhealthy conditions.

What are automatic thoughts or automatic assumptions?

Automatic assumptions or core beliefs are your views of the world that were acquired during your childhood. Your experiences as a child will form your automatic thoughts.

Typically, you overestimate the threat, imagining it to be so big that you underestimate your capability to cope with that threat. Your views of situations around you are distorted because of this.

Example

During your childhood you drowned in a swimming pool and you almost died. You were brought to the ER of your local hospital. The shrieking of the ambulance's siren, the cries of your parents, and the shouts of the medical team had left an unforgettable imprint in your mind.

Since then, you hated swimming pools, and you tremble every time you happen to go near one. You perceive that all swimming pools will drown you, and that they are always unsafe. These are distorted views or dysfunctional thoughts you have because of your core belief.

What to do:

You should work on these automatic assumptions and dysfunctional thoughts so you can change the way you think about them, and consequently, change the way you behave and act.

In the process of changing these dysfunctional thoughts, you should strive to maintain a positive frame of mind. Optimism is the key for the success of CBT,

You must learn how to challenge your automatic thoughts, and practice your CBY skills continuously.

You should also accomplish your thought journal daily and consistently. Always challenge automatic thoughts, so you gradually change your dysfunctional thoughts and behavior. Remember to monitor your progress regularly.

What I think, what I feel, what I do – are all interconnected. Thus, your automatic thoughts, which are dysfunctional or distorted, will produce negative behavior and emotions.

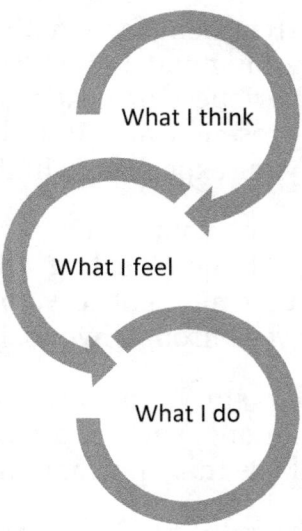

You can think of the relationship of these 3 aspects of your personality as irrevocable. They're meant to be interlinked together – forever. When you can understand this, you can understand CBT better.

Chapter 2: History of Cognitive Behavioral Therapy

The evolution of Cognitive Behavioral Therapy (CBT) started in the 1900s as practitioners explored other means of treating mental disorders and behavioral reactions. The history can be divided in three phases:

The Psychoanalytic Therapy era (1800 to 1900)

In the 1800s, this treatment for emotional and mental illness was popularized by Sigmund Freud. This therapy focused on early childhood experiences or past experiences that affect an individual in the present time. It is believed that your life today is a result of your experiences in the past.

It is done by unearthing your past experiences by allowing you to talk about your past and revealing what you felt and thought when you were at that moment in your life. This information can be drawn from you through hypnosis.

While you tell your story, the therapist intently listens to determine which among your experiences is affecting your current life. He will use this information to treat you.

The Cognitive Therapy Period (1940 to 1979)

In the 1940s, Alfred Alder an Austrian Psychotherapist infused cognition in psychotherapy which is based on the belief of Hans Vaihinger, a Kantian that individuals create their own philosophy and rules to allow them to understand their world based on their experiences.

Valinger said that these principles can be the product of the imagination, or it may be fiction, which later could become the conviction of an individual due to the constant use.

Alder's theory is that a person's emotional troubles emanate from his thoughts. The emotions or reactions of an individual to a situation are highly dependent on how he perceives the situation or event. This prompted a shift from usual psychotherapy treatment to Cognitive.

Based on the theory of Alder, Aaron T. Beck, came up with an approach called cognitive therapy. Since human beings are a thinking lot with rational minds, it is expected that you can control your emotions, behavior and your thoughts.

This recognition of the cognitive aspect of a human being, ushered in the cognitive therapy used by (Mahoney, 1974; Meichenbaum, 1977; Shaw, Rush & Emery, 1979)

The treatment adopts the idea that you can manage your emotions, unpleasant thoughts and behavior to avoid anxiety. You can work with the therapist to find a way for you to alter your behavior from bad to good, reduce your tendencies for negative and twisted thoughts and develop a good mind set for a better you.

Through the years the therapy took on changes to enhance the techniques and concepts utilized by practitioners.

The Cognitive Behavioral Therapy (1974 onwards)

The treatment for mental conditions scaled up with the combination of the psychoanalysis and cognitive approaches referred to as cognitive behavioral therapy (CBT), which is now used to treat varied mental illnesses.

It must be emphasized that CBT adopts the three-pronged concept of the interconnection of the mind, emotion and behavior.

It focuses on looking at your situation or the condition you are in at the moment, studying your thoughts and emotions, how you are physically feeling and how you act at a given situation.

This therapy is set on developing strategies that can help patients cope up with their mental and behavioral problems. The therapy adopts a four-stage approach: Assessment and Evaluation, Skills build up, skills sustainability and Follow through or post evaluation stage.

On evaluation and assessment, you are subjected to a battery of psychological examinations to have a closer look into your personality, thoughts, behavior and other crucial aspects of your being. This stage is meant to understand you as a person and come up with a technique on how you can behave more positively or appropriately.

On skills build up and sustainability, you are taught to learn the many coping strategies that you can use to improve on how you react to certain situations and how to overcome pervert thoughts. You are to undertake continuing capacity build up and sustain the skills you have acquired.

On the post evaluation and assessment stage, you will be evaluated again after the treatments have been done to determine your progress. It will access the problematic and success areas of your treatment. The results could be for re-engineering your approach and to sustain the successful ones.

CBT has been on the forefront of mental illnesses' treatment for decades, and continue to be a universal approach in treating mental problems.

Chapter 3: Understanding the Power of the Mind

Cognitive Behavioral Therapy relies on the power of the mind to cause changes in the way a person thinks, behaves and acts.

Almost everyone is aware of the reported power of the mind, but only few persons actually believe in it, while you can count with your fingers people who are using this power to change their lives positively and discover their hidden potentials.

Why so? It's because they don't firmly believe in the principle that the mind has control over the body, and that the mind can control the way a person acts and behaves.

This belief dates back to the Christian era, when Jesus Christ declared to his disciples:

"Truly I tell you, if you have faith as small as a mustard seed, you can say to this mountain, 'Move from here to there,' and it will move. Nothing will be impossible for you."

That's the power of the mind revealed by one of the most popular figures in Christianity. For people during that era, all they need to do was to believe that the mountain can move, and it will. It's a mind-blowing thought to imagine the mountain actually moving just because you told it so.

It defies what we normally know about objects. Our humanity had categorized things into stereotypes. "I cannot move that because it's a mountain."

But the statement came from someone, who had walked on water. Hence, it can be done.

Okay, so you don't want to know more about Christianity. What about the legendary Master Yoda in "Star Wars", who said:

"Try not, do or do not."

Yoda said this when Luke Skywalker wasn't able to lift the X-string Starfighter out from the lake using his mind.

When Luke said, *"I cannot do it."*

Master Yoda replied:

"It's only in your mind."

This story is a work of fiction, but the concept that the power of the mind is limitless is demonstrated in this scene.

You're still unconvinced? What about this: the Placebo Effect.

Placebo Effect

The Placebo Effect was seen in clinical trials when drugs were tested for their effectiveness. The placebo pill was included to ensure that results were valid.

The placebo is also called the 'dummy pill' because it doesn't contain the components of the drug being tested.

Researchers had found out that when the control individuals (those who took the Placebo pill) believed that they had taken the genuine drug, they had experienced the same effects as those who took the genuine pill. There are numerous studies that have proven the Placebo Effect.

These results indicate that what the mind thinks, the body will respond accordingly.

Thoughts of pregnancy and sickness

There were several reports too of persons thinking firmly they were pregnant or sick, and their bodies, indeed, demonstrated the symptoms of pregnancy or sickness.

Multiple Personality Disorder/Split Personality Disorder

In addition, the power of the mind can be demonstrated in personality disorders, and doctors are still perplexed at how different unique personalities are found in one body.

The most intriguing fact is that the physiological and physical characteristics of each personality differ from one another.

Example:

A dual personality exists in Dave. The first personality is Kevin, who is a diabetic with poor eyesight. The other personality is Alex, who is sporty and healthy.

When the personality of Kevin surfaces, the person (Dave) truly shows the symptoms of a diabetic; his blood sugar shoots up (hyperglycemia), and he needs to use eyeglasses to read.

When the personality of Alex takes over, the blood sugar returns to normal and the poor eyesight is gone. Every personality trait of Kevin disappears like magic, and these shows a direct link from the mind to the body; that anything the mind believes in can be accomplished by the body.

This goes true with the other personalities present in that person. Researchers noticed that even the eye color, posture, manner of speaking and other traits of the person with multiple personality disorder changed, every time a new personality takes over.

The surprising thing is that the multiple personalities inside the person with psychological illness don't 'know' each other.

Isn't that amazing? But, wouldn't it be awesome too, if you can command your body to do impossible things that are good to humankind using your normal mind?

Telekinesis and Mental Telepathy

There are reports too about rare individuals proven to have telekinetic and telepathic powers. Both of these powers are controlled by the mind.

These are undeniable and empirical proofs that if the mind is set – unwaveringly in a thought - it can be powerful enough to cause changes in the body. The mind can control your body and your actions, thoughts and behavior.

Surely, the point is proven by the Placebo Effect's clinical trials done by countless of drug companies and scientists; the power of the mind of persons with multiple personality disorder and those with super powers.

There are documented cases of individuals being able to miraculously cure themselves through your mental prowess.

But why are people not stoked in using their mental powers?

It's because it takes dedication, concentration, diligence, patience, and hard work to develop the powers of the brain.

Every person has this mental power, only in varying degrees. Yours can be dormant because you haven't used it for years.

Aside from these scientific findings, physiologically, the brain has also the main function of governing the body. When you're unconscious, you won't be feeling anything, because the brain cannot recognize and acknowledge the stimuli.

The stimulus has to be recognized and acknowledged first by the brain before the body can react. Let's discuss more about the functions of the brain related to our topic.

Physiology of the Brain

The brain is the center of the Central Nervous System. The hypothalamus, in particular, is responsible in releasing and inhibiting hormones to respond to the body's need after a stimulus is received.

An example is when the body is low in thyroid hormones (hypothyroidism), this stimulus will trigger the brain to release Thyrotropin Releasing Factor (TRF) or Thyrotropin Releasing Hormone (TRH) to the thyroid glands.

TRF triggers the thyroid glands to increase the secretion of the thyroid hormones (T3 and T4), until the concentration goes back to normal.

When it does, the normal levels of the hormone will be fed again to the brain, and the brain will decrease the release of TRH, and TRH will decrease the secretion of the thyroid hormones.

This is only one of the hormones that the hypothalamus secretes. The rest of the major hormones secreted by the hypothalamus are:

- **Growth Hormone Releasing Hormone (GHRH)** – controls growth and development of the body.
- **Corticotropin Releasing Hormone (CRH) or Corticotropin Releasing Factor (CRF)** – triggers the adrenal cortex to secrete cortisol
- **Gonadotropin Releasing Hormone (GnRH)** – responsible for the gonads, the reproductive organs of the body
- **Somatostatin** (GHIH) – inhibits the release of Growth Hormone and Thyroid Stimulating Hormone
- **Oxytocin** – produced by the hypothalamus and helps in the birthing process. It is primarily released by the posterior pituitary.
- **Anti-diuretic hormone (ADH) or vasopressin** – helps in the water balance by retention of water, and is primarily released by the posterior pituitary gland.

Therefore, when the hypothalamus doesn't recognize the stimulus send by any part of the body, there will be no corresponding reaction.

Did you have some experiences similar to these occurrences? Was there a time in your life when you wanted to get sick, and you did get sick later on? Did you experience calling up a family member because you remembered him? You found out eventually that he was thinking of you.

This confirms the conclusion that there's an essential connection of the mind to how your body operates. How you feel, react and behave has a scientific basis and is not merely hearsay.

Chapter 4: Know Thyself, a Self-Assessment

We have established the undeniable connection of the brain to how your body reacts, feels and behaves. Your next step now is to assess yourself and get to know yourself better.

This is a necessary step because you cannot move forward if you don't have any idea what weaknesses and strengths you have. In order to improve yourself, you have to know what trait you should develop.

Here's a step by step process you can follow.

Step #1 – Choose a quiet and secure place.

Your room is the best place to conduct this activity. You can lie down or stay seated, whichever makes you more comfortable. Regulate the temperature of the room, so it's not too cold or too warm.

Wear comfortable clothing, without tight areas that can constrict your movement. Be ready with a pen and paper. It's recommended that you used a logbook, so you can use it for the entire CBT process.

Step #2 – Perform breathing exercises.

Before the actual activity, perform some breathing exercises to stabilize your body. Sit, yoga-lotus style, with your legs crossed, each of the feet are placed on the opposite thigh, with the sole facing upwards and the heel facing towards the abdomen.

You can rest your hands on the edges of your lap - palms up, or positioned them on top of each other at the center of your body. Some people prefer to link their thumb and index finger - but it's not necessary. See image below.

Lotus Position

This lotus position allows the smooth flow of energy within your body, stabilizing it more quickly.

Of course, if you cannot perform this position, it's okay. You can sit in the most comfortable position, as long as you maintain the correct posture: your back straight, shoulder blades are in line with the pelvis on both sides, and not jutting forward.

Step #3 – Breathe in and breathe out

Breathe in deeply through your nose, with your mouth closed, and then breathe out slowly through your mouth. Do these several times until you feel your muscles relax and your respiration becoming even.

Step #4 – Recall the instances that you have experienced fear and anxiety

Go over your experiences in your mind. What made you most fearful and anxious? Why? Take note of your worst fears. What were the effects of your fears?

Step #5 – Recall the instances that you have experienced anger and depression

Go over your experiences with anger and depression and try to remember them. What were the causes of your anger? What were the causes of your depression? Were you able to recover from them? Take note of the answers to these questions.

Step #6 – Recall any other feelings that have disturbed your peace of mind

What other emotions caused you pain? Take note of the reasons and the magnitude of that emotion. What happened afterwards? Were you able to overcome your feelings? What helped you overcome them? Write down the answers.

Step #7 – Open your eyes and slowly disengage from your lotus position

Don't make abrupt movements. On your logbook, write down the occurrences that you have previously recalled. Tabulate and rank your fears and worries according to the magnitude of the emotions that you have felt. This can represent your Hierarchy of Feared Situations.

Example

Table 1

Rank	Distress 0-10	Specific Situation	Did you avoid it?
1	10	Speaking before a big crowd	Yes
2	7	Being embarrassed in public	Yes
3	7	Meeting an 'enemy' in the	Yes

		street	
4	6	Fear of open spaces	Yes
5	6	Fear of the future	Not possible
6	6	Fear of losing friends	Yes
7	5	Fear of separation from family	Yes

Step #8 – Assess your fears according to their effects

Create another table to assess whether your fears did pan out or not.

Table 2

Specific Situation	Worst that could happen	Did it happen?	Ways to recover
Speaking before a big crowd	You become speechless because of fear	Not yet done	Gradual exposure to crowds
Being embarrassed in public	Your friend or family member embarrassing you in public	no	Get over the fear
Meeting an 'enemy' in the street	You exchange heated words	no	Believe in yourself
Fear of open spaces	You might feel dizzy and uncomfortable	yes	Gradual exposure
Fear of the future	Afraid to die and to get sick	no	Stop worrying
Fear of losing friends	The fear becoming a reality	no	Stop worrying
Fear of separation from family	The fear becoming a	no	Stop worrying

	reality		

If you go over the fears listed above, most of them are needless fears, such as fear of the future, fear of losing friends, and fear of separation. You cannot worry about the future, which you don't have total control of. This could drive you crazy.

You must have faith that the future will be good to you. Worrying about it will not add a day to your life.

The best thing that you can do in such circumstances is to do the best you can and stop worrying about things you cannot control.

Your present time is wasted because you spend time worrying about the next days to come. You spend your life in fear never getting over it. What a devastating way to spend your precious life.

The discovery of your worst fears identifies you as a person, who is weak when it comes to controlling your fears. These are considered your weaknesses.

Step #9 - Take note of your weaknesses

You can base your weakness from your step #8. Write them down.

Example

Table 3

Weaknesses	Intensity 0-10	Ways to overcome	Results Date/ Done – √ Not Done –

			X
Lack of self-confidence	9	>Improve one's self through reading > learn new skills > psyche self, daily > acquire a new hobby	8/1 - √ 8/1 - X 8/1 - √ 8/1 - √
Afraid of social interaction	9	>Go out more >Acquire new friends >Visit places where social interaction is required (parties, picnics)	
Being a pushover	8	>Learn how to say 'No' >when you're right, put your foot down.	
Lack of patience	7	>Learn how to wait >Practice the virtue every day	

You can also omit the "Results" column from the table above and create a new table for monitoring your improvement.

Example

Table 4

Date	Weaknesses	Coping	Done – √

		Mechanism	Not Done – X
8/1	Lack of self-confidence	>Improve one's self through reading > learn new skills > psyche self, daily > acquire a new hobby	
	Afraid of social interaction	>Go out more >Acquire new friends >Visit places where social interaction is required (parties, picnics)	
	Being a pushover	>Learn how to say 'No' >when you're right, put your foot down.	
	Lack of patience	>Learn how to wait >Practice the virtue every day	

You can prepare your weakness and remedies table every day. Naturally, the entries can be different from the entries here, but more or less this is one way of constructing your table. You can modify the table to suit your preferences.

Request family members and friends to describe you weaknesses in 3 words. You may want to include them in your list, if you find them valid. Have an open mind because the perception of other people may vary from your perception of yourself.

Example

- o   Insecure, moody, lazy
- o   Fat, ugly, crazy

Step #10 – Take note of your strengths

These are the positive traits that you have. Write down your strengths and grade them according to how dominant that trait is.

Example

Table 5

Strengths	Intensity 0-10	Ways to maintain them	Results Date/ Done – √ Not Done – X
Diligent	10	>Maintain good quality of work	8/1 - √
Good in graphic designing	9	>search for more exposure	
Helpful	9	>Continue helping other people. Daily Target: 1 stranger	

		helped	
Generous	7	>Continue being generous	

You should also ask your family members and friends to describe you positively, using three words.

Examples

- o   Jolly, amiable, witty
- o   Prudent, faithful, trustworthy

Step #11 - Collate all the information you have collected from this activity

Collate all the data that you have collected from this activity and summarize your findings in a table:

Example

Table 6

Table of personality traits

Strengths	Weaknesses	Comments
Diligent	Lack of self-confidence	
Good in graphic designing	Afraid of social interaction	
Helpful	Being a pushover	
Generous	Lack of patience	
Jolly	Insecure	
Amiable	Moody	
Witty	Lazy	

Now you have a bird's eye-view of who you are. From this information you can proceed to develop your personality for the better.

Bear in mind that in CBT, the focus is on acquiring a positive frame of mind through practice.

Chapter 5: What You Think is What You Are

Mind over matter: *"what you think is what you are."* If you're still not familiar with this slogan, inculcate this phrase now in your mind.

As you have learned from chapter 2, the mind is the super-organ of the body that can control everything in your body. It has been scientifically proven, over and over.

Now, you can take advantage of this power by believing firmly in it and using it to change your life forever.

A similar slogan is *"If you think you can, you can."*

Hence, if you think you're self-confident, then you are. This goes without saying that you should be willing to do the accompanying hard work to achieve the behavior that you desire.

However, you have to change the way you think first. That's why it's important that you should believe in yourself.

Create a new table and list the weaknesses that you have discovered in chapter 3. and opposite it write the trait that can counter that weakness.

Use your logbook for all of these activities, so you won't lose any pages.

Example

Table 7

Weaknesses	Target Behavior
Lack of self-confidence	Confident
Afraid of social interaction	Likes social interaction
Being a pushover	Firm

Lack of patience	Patient
Insecure	Secure
Moody	Stable
Lazy	Industrious

The target behavior is the behavior that you would like to attain. There are no complex tricks – just a firm belief that you can do it (faith), and the patience and dedication to practice the behavior every day. *"Fake it until you have it."*

Act as if you're confident and eventually you will acquire that behavior. You might say that these are all generalities, and you don't know exactly how to do it.

Hence, here's a step by step explanation of how to do it.

How to overcome your weaknesses

Step #1 – Change the way you think

Every time you think that you lack self-confidence, you're feeding that weakness in you. You're letting it grow and rule your personality. You are your worst enemy. Once you recognize this, vow to yourself to never let this happen again.

Psyching yourself every day can help in eschewing the negative thought in your mind. This will introduce the idea to your subconscious mind. When both your subconscious and conscious mind become aware of the thought – you will quickly acquire that positive trait.

Every morning when you wake up, look at the mirror and affirm to yourself the positive behavior that you want to cultivate.

Example

"I'm self-confident. I love social interaction. I'm firm, patient, secure, stable and industrious."

Look at yourself in the mirror and state the positive statements above. You can say it loudly and slowly, so your mind will absorb the thought completely. If there are people in the room, then you can say it mentally.

Relax your body, and do this a couple of times so that the thought would sink in. If you have time to spare, doing it while meditating is also a good practice.

Perform this ritual twice a day: right after you wake up, and then before you retire in the night.

If you find it overwhelming to combine all the positive traits together you can do it one by one. You can start with self-confidence first. Doing it one by one would also allow you to perform visualization.

Doing Visualization

After you have said to yourself several times, *"I am confident."*

You can practice visualization. Visualize yourself talking in front of people confidently. Imagine how you would walk into the front with your confident strides, your back straight and your shoulders relaxed. Visualize every single, confident movement that you would make.

Visualize yourself talking confidently, your voice strong and clear, your eyes looking straight at your audience. Then visualize yourself walking back to your seat amidst the applause of the audience.

Step #2 – Walk the talk

Act out your visualization. Act confident even if you're still trying to. Again, *"you are what you think you are"*. If you're still trembling in your boots, get rid of the thought as soon as it enters your mind.

You're a confident person, thus, you must act confident. It can be difficult at first, but as your subconscious absorbs the thoughts, your actions will become more natural. Before you know it, you have indeed become a self-confident person.

Step #3 – Repeat the process until you have developed all of the positive traits

It's easier said than done, but it can be done. Mind over matter. Nothing is impossible to the determined mind. Do, there is no try. Reinforce these beliefs over and over until it becomes automatic to you.

In these steps, the power of the mind is again emphasized. You cannot do anything without the mind. You can turn your weaknesses into strength, if you think you can.

You can do it!

Chapter 6: Understanding Your Fear and Anxiety

Together with the development of your character, you should also conquer your fear and anxiety. You may have noticed that your fear and anxiety have prevented you to venture into unknown territory.

Because of this, you withdraw into your own shell. You became moody, anxious and depressed. You had become psychologically unhinged. For you to conquer your fear and anxiety, you have to understand them first.

Keep in mind that you are fearful, not because of what happened, but because of how you interpreted what happened. Your interpretation had made all the difference.

When you change your thoughts, your feelings, behavior and reactions will change, as well.

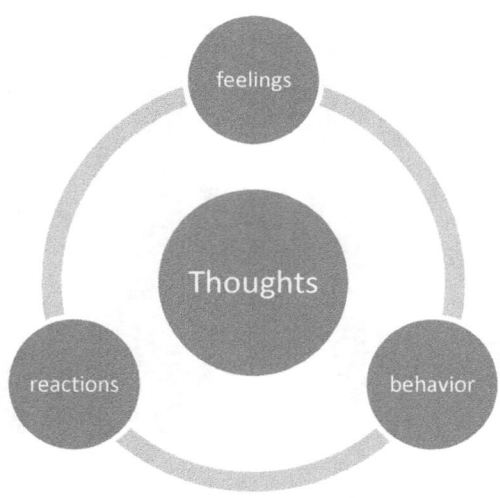

<u>Here are facts about fear and anxiety that you must know.</u>

➢ **Fear and anxiety are natural.**

You're not human if you don't experience fear and anxiety. These are natural and normal feelings that humans undergo. An ample amount of fear and anxiety is good. They prevent people in committing mistakes and injustices. They motivate people to do better. They make people be more cautious and ingenious.

However, they should not control you because if they do, you cannot live a happy and contented life.

➢ **Fear and anxiety can make you act irrationally.**

When you're anxious and in fear; you usually act irrationally. The perceived threat can drive you to commit acts, which you don't typically do. Some of your actions don't make sense to other people because they simply don't.

An example is when you refuse to budge from your house because of your fear of people. Your fear can be justified at times, but it's excessive. You become immobilized by your fear, and you have isolated yourself from people.

➢ **Most of your fears and the things you're anxious about are unfounded.**

If you look long enough at the list of your fears and the things you're anxious about, you will notice that most of them are unfounded.

Let's prove that this is true. In your logbook, create a table of your feared situations.

Example

Table 8

Assessment of Feared Situations

Date	Feared Situations	Anxiety rating (before) 0-10	Anxiety rating (during) 0-10	Anxiety rating (after) 0-10	Length of time in minutes	Reactions Comment Observations
8/1	Social interaction	10	10	8	60	>It was not so scary after all >enjoyed talking to Tom >will be less scared next time

You can break down the social interaction into specific events, so you can manage your fears more accurately.

Example

Specific social interaction activities

- o Birthday party
- o Acquaintance party
- o Group discussions

- Company's R & R (rest and recreation)

You can write these activities in your table and evaluate accordingly. You will notice that most of your fears or imagined threats don't come to fruition.

Tabulate your other fears too, and assess the results. From there, you can now establish a factual basis for your fears and anxiety.

- **Excessive fear and anxiety can prevent you from doing great things.**

    Because of your fear of something, you may avoid doing things that can, otherwise, be beneficial to you. If you don't accept the challenge of conquering your fear and doing new things, you can never develop your full potential.

    Example

    You were chosen by your group to be the team leader, but because you fear that you may not able to lead the group, you refused the responsibility. In refusing this, your leadership skills will not be developed and you'll never learn how to be a leader.

    You have missed a superb opportunity to hone your leadership skills, just because of your fear.

- **You will fear most and be anxious about that which you don't know.**

    People fear what they don't know, and that's normal. Even the bravest persons are fearful of what they are not familiar with. Nevertheless, you have to overcome this fear by attempting to know the unknown.

This is the reason why scientists continue to research and experiment on unknown things, so humans would know more, and be less fearful.

- **Unfounded fears and unnecessary anxiety (imagined threats) can prevent you from living a normal life.**

You cannot live a normal life if you fear almost everything. As previously mentioned, fear is natural and normal – BUT – don't allow this fear to control you.

You have to master your own feelings, such as fear, anxiety, anger and depression. Keep in mind that you have full possession of your body and behavior through your mind, Hence, use this 'weapon' effectively. You can, if you think you can.

- **The natural response of the body to fear is to secrete more stress hormones.**

The brain (mind) controls your body. When the brain recognizes that the body is in danger because of the feeling of fear that was fed to the hypothalamus, the brain commands the adrenal medulla to secrete the 'emergency hormones' or stress hormones called catecholamine.

The catecholamine hormones provide extra energy for the body to "fight or flight" (face the fear or run away from it.)

The body's responses:

- Blood circulation increases
- Heart rate increases
- Respiration increases
- Muscular strength increases
- Glucose metabolism increases

- Blood pressure increases

The body's automatic response will help you cope with the perceived threat (fear).

There are countless documented cases of persons being able to do extraordinary feats during such incidences. An example is when one man can carry a big freezer during a fire, but cannot carry the same freezer after the emergency has been resolved.

> **You can control your fear and anxiety by changing the way you think.**

This is the most important fact that you should remember, once you change your negative attitude, by starting to think positively, all your fears will diminish.

Cognitive Distortions and what to do

These are distortions of the truth by your faulty ways of thinking. Falsity can appear true to people with this mental condition. In this state, your mind distorts the falsehood so that you think it's true.

Go over these examples, and determine if you're a victim of cognitive distortions. You must avoid these cognitive distortions, if you want to get rid of these psychological disorders and fears, and get your life back.

1. **Overgeneralization**

    This type of cognitive distortion is when you base your general conclusions on just one experience. For example you went to Dallas for an IT conference, and you were billeted in a hotel where the desk staff members were unfriendly. You then conclude that all staff members of hotels in Dallas are unfriendly.

This is a distorted cognitive view because the conclusion is not accurate. Of course, not all hotel employees in Dallas hotels are unfriendly.

But that's how people sometimes think. You may think this way too.

What do you think of the conclusion? Did you notice that it's distorted? How can you conclude that way when you still have not visited the other hotels?

What to do

If you can recognize the cognitive distortion in this example, then that's good for you. What you can do now, is not to commit the same mistake. You should refrain from overgeneralization because it's unfair and wrong. If you're not sure of your data or perception, don't conclude.

2. Filtering

This happens when you 'filter' the good and only retain all the bad. Often, you automatically focus on all the bad things in your life and ignore the many good things in your life. It's a flawed perception but many people do this.

They complain about their jobs, their children, their house. They complain about almost anything. But they fail to see the good things around them: how healthy and beautiful their kids are; how good the weather is; how they have sufficient money to buy the things they want; how they have a complete body. They don't appreciate what they have.

What to do

You must learn how to do it the other way around. Think only of the good things and ignore the bad things. When you get use to this cognitive exercise, you will find out that there are more 'positives' than 'negatives' around you.

Learning to appreciate is one way of being able to perceive only the good things. Say "thank you" to your spouse for cooking dinner for you. Be thankful for whatever you have.

3. **Jumping to conclusions**

You may often jump to conclusions without proof. You conclude hastily, without researching or finding out the truth. This is harmful because you can hurt other people.

What to do

Refrain from concluding without any proof. Even with proof, don't use your knowledge to harm other people. Don't be judgmental because the yardstick that you use to measure other people will be the same yardstick that will be used to measure you.

4. **Personalization**

If you have this cognitive distortion, you will think that things go wrong because of you. You blame yourself for the negative things that happen to others – even if you're not responsible for it. An example is when you blame yourself for the failure of an activity, simply because you were a member of the organizers.

This is an extremely distorted view. It shows how your self-confidence is so low that you practically blame yourself all the time.

What to do

Give yourself credit. As previously mentioned, think of the opposite positive thought and concentrate on it. Go over the situation and analyze if you have direct connection to what went wrong.

You should reframe your thoughts to:

"I'm not the cause of the failure. I have helped in organizing the activity but I did my part well. There may be some other factors that contributed to the failure."

You may have some responsibility, but it's not entirely your fault. Don't castigate yourself for a mistake that you may not have committed.

5. **Depersonalization**

This is when you put all the blame on other people when it's entirely your responsibility. You think you're not good enough because of other people, so you blame them for your inadequacy.

What to do

Think rationally. Was it your responsibility to do the task or not? If you are part of the team, then you're responsible too.

Nonetheless, if all of you and your officemates are in-charge of the activity, both of you must share the responsibility, and no one must be singled out. You must strike a balance when to assume responsibility and when not to.

6. Looking glass

You may have a looking glass distortion when you tend to magnify or minimize something.

Just like using a looking glass, perceptions can be distorted according to how the looking glass is held.

What to do

Negative things must not be magnified, but positive things should be. Bear in mind that it won't benefit you if you keep harping about the negative things in your life.

Example

The teacher showed the class a white paper with a dot at the center. She asked the class to describe the paper.

Almost everyone wrote. *"There's a dot in the center of the paper."*

Only two students wrote: *"It's a white sheet of paper with a small smudge."*

That's usually how humans think. They concentrate on the bad and ignore the good.

The teacher told them:

Many of you didn't notice the white sheet of paper that's unblemished, but notice the one, dark spot. From now on, reframe your mind to look for the good and beautiful only.

Whatever cognitive distortions you have in your life, you can do away with them, if you're determined to. Again, nothing is impossible to the determined mind.

Your fears won't disappear, for sure, but you will be able to deal with them in a positive way, and not the other way around. They will serve as your stepping stones towards your success in living a normal life.

Chapter 7: Setting Your Goals in Resolving Your Fears and Anxieties

At this point, you're now ready to set your goals in resolving your fears and anxieties. The purpose of setting your short term and long term goals is to provide a clear blueprint or map of where you are going.

Without clear goals, you may waste your time meandering and guessing what to do next. Nonetheless, before you set your goals, you must have already acknowledged that the mind is a powerful tool in overcoming your fears.

You must have inculcated in your mind that the way you think can control how you behave and act. If not, then you have to go back to the first chapters and read about the power of your mind. Psyche yourself until you truly believe in it.

After this necessary phase, you can proceed to the next step.

Setting you goals

In setting your goals, you can use the SMART method. SMART stands for Specific, Measurable, Attainable, Relevant and Time Bound.

Of course, you can always modify them so that your goals will be in congruent with your needs. There are no identical cases because each person is unique.

What does SMART mean?

Specific

Your goals must be specific and clearly defined. Avoid generalizations. When your goals are specific, you can quickly verify them.

Examples

- At the end of the therapy, I would be able to conquer the fear of open spaces.
- At the end of the therapy, I would be able to walk alone to the train station.
- At the end of the therapy, I would be able to cross the street on my own.

Measurable

You can measure or quantify the results or effects readily. Without this aspect, you cannot determine if your goals have been achieved or not. So, set goals that you can measure.

Examples

- At the end of the therapy, I would be able to walk alone to the train station 10 times.
- At the end of the therapy, I would be able to cross the street on my own twice a day.

Attainable

Set goals that you can attain. Avoid goals that are impossible to achieve.

Examples

- At the end of the therapy, I would be able to mingle among people during parties.
- At the end of the therapy, I would be able to express myself during our monthly company meetings.

Relevant

Your goal should be relevant to the existing community around you. Does your goal contribute something positive to others? Does your goal work in the present time?

Examples

- At the end of the therapy, I would be able to join volunteers to help other people with the same fears as my own.
- At the end of the therapy, I would be able to help my friends overcome their own fears.

Based on these guidelines, you can now prepare your own goals. Take note that these are your personal goals, so they must be geared towards your own development and conquest of your own fears.

Examples

Overall Therapy Goals

At the end of the therapy, I would be able to:

- Talk in public every time I am asked to.
- Socialize with people within my circle every day.
- Stay in open spaces whenever I am out with family and friends.

In your logbook, write down all the fears that you have identified so far. Be specific with your fears, so you can prepare specific goals that you could achieve. Prepare goals for each of these fears and anxieties.

These two terms are connected, thus, you can create a goal for both of them.

Example

When you fear heights, your anxieties would be: you're anxious that you might fall, you're anxious that you might jump off, and so forth. Therefore, you can create one goal for your fear and anxieties because they refer to the same fear.

Long-term goal

At the end of the therapy, I would be able to go up the stairs of buildings without assistance.

You could also create short term goals to be able to monitor your progress quickly.

Example

At the end of 1 month, I would be able to:

- Express myself to my family and close friends.
- Socialize with 10 people within my circle.
- Stay in open spaces for 1 hour.

You can adapt the method you're most comfortable with. Remember the end point is for you to eliminate your dysfunctional thoughts/automatic thoughts to more realistic and more positive thoughts.

Chapter 8: Implementing Your Goals for Fear and Anxiety Management

In this chapter, you will be learning how to implement your goals in order to manage your fear and anxiety. There are steps that you have to follow, so you can easily monitor your progress.

You can start by managing the fear that is easiest to conquer. After conquering that fear, you can proceed to the other fears you want to overcome.

Step #1 – Identify your fears

In your logbook, take note of the fears that you have listed there. Create a new table and write them down one by one.

Step #2 – Identify the steps you need to implement

Identify the steps you need to implement to conquer your fears. What specific steps should you do to accomplish this? You should prepare steps that you can perform by yourself. The steps should be in chronological order.

Step #3 – Identify effective coping mechanisms for each of your fears

What coping mechanisms or strategies can be effective for each of your fears? These can differ from person to person. Thus, it can help, if you devise your coping mechanisms by yourself. This is because you have an inkling – more or less - which ones may be effective or not for you. Also, use all useful resources.

If you cannot come up with coping mechanisms, you can experiment and find out what works best for you. Keep exploring strategies until you find a coping mechanism that can work for you.

Step #4 - Evaluate the results.

After implementing the coping mechanisms you can evaluate the results if there's a change in the degree of anxiety for each of your fears. What coping mechanism worked effectively? What did not work? What would you do differently next time?

A sample table would look like this:

Table 9

Date	Fear	Steps to implement	Coping Mechanisms	Evaluation
8/01	Public speaking	>Step 1 - speak to a small groups (family and friends) practice for 1 month. >Step 2 - speak to larger groups (office groups) practice for 1 month >Step 3 - speak in	>daily interaction with family >moral support from family, such as words of encouragement	The daily family interaction worked well, but step 3 was difficult to do. Solution: More exposure for step 1 & 2 before exposure to step 3.

| | | front of a big audience | | |

The first fear listed in the table above is public speaking, which is the most common fear many people have. You can change this entry to accommodate your own fears.

You can also use this table to provide more space to write on.

Table 10

Type of Fear
Steps to implement
Coping mechanism
Evaluation

Notes

Start with the fear that is easiest for you to manage. Then gradually cope with your other fears. You have to conquer your fears one at a time, so you can focus. It would be difficult to cope with all of your fears simultaneously.

Your expected reactions to your feared situations can be any of these following safety behaviors:

➢ **Avoidance of feared situations** – instead of being anxious, you try to avoid such situations. This can be bad because you cannot avoid your fear forever. You have to expose yourself, gradually. You can do it, just be persistent.

➢ **Seeking reassurance from others** – you could always run to your family and friends for reassurance but they will not be forever available for you. There will come a time that they will leave you, and where will you go then? With the guidance of this book, you can conquer your fear for good.

Seek reassurance from yourself instead and everything will turn out well.

- **Over preparation** – you check repeatedly to make sure everything is in order. You're overdoing it, stressing everybody. You may double check your preparation, but doing it several times is exaggerated.

  Control yourself in overdoing it. Don't be a slave-master.

- **Procrastination** – you procrastinate because you're afraid your fear might come true. But mind you, only a few of your fears will come true. Don't torture yourself by your dysfunctional thoughts.

- **Perfectionism** – you don't want anything to go wrong, so you want everything to be perfect. Nothing is perfect in this world. Thus, loosen up and relax your grip on your fear.

Coming up with coping mechanisms

In the coping mechanisms, you can brainstorm first to obtain all ideas possible. Don't filter any idea. Write them all down. What may seem to be an irrelevant idea might actually be the coping mechanism that can work later.

Explore all the coping mechanisms that you have come up with and experiment with them one-by-one.

Gradual exposure

You can also do gradual exposure. As you get exposed to your fears, you can eventually conquer them. This method can help cure your fears and phobias.

Steps of gradual exposure

1. Psyche yourself positively by confirming to yourself that your phobia is unnatural. Until you're sure of your mental state, don't attempt to expose yourself.

2. Face your fear gradually. Do it slowly.

   Example:

   You have fear of walking on side roads

   For the first day, you can stand at the side road for a few minutes. Observe your behavior. Reframe your mind that there's nothing wrong in walking on side roads.

   On the second day, you can take a few steps forward. Walk that length of the road, back and forth. Do this several days until your behavior is not extreme. You can ask someone to accompany you.
   On the third day, you can increase the distance. Do this until your behavior becomes normal.

Self-soothing

You can soothe yourself through self-psyching. You can tell yourself soothing words and words of encouragement to eliminate the negative thoughts.

In alarm responses, the following are established.

1. **Your perception of the threat** – whether the threat is external, internal, or merely a conditioned threat, you may have become aware of it. Hence, an alarm button is pressed in your head.

2. **Your appraisal of the threat** – are you able to appraise the threat correctly? Let's say you are threatened by a raging river. Does the river threaten your domicile? How high is it? How strong is the current?

3. **Physiological and emotional response** – you would hyperventilate because of fear. Your blood pressure would elevate, and your pulses will quicken. Your emergency

hormones, such as epinephrine, will also be increased in secretion. This hormone will further elevate your blood sugar and your muscles become stronger.

The body responds to your thoughts. Because you think there's a threat, the physiology of the body reacts. You may even get sick if your mind doesn't stop thinking a threat exists.

4. **Behavioral response**

   You may run away from the raging river and shout for help. You may also climb to higher places to ensure that you won't be washed away by the strong current.

   In this case, your behavior was dictated by your mind.

How long will you use the steps and the table?

There's no limit. You can use it as often as you can. You should use it to conquer one particular fear at a time until you have conquered all your fears. You can modify the steps or the coping mechanism based on your evaluation of what worked and what didn't work from your first exposure.

You can perform the steps again, omitting strategies that didn't work and including strategies that worked, and new ones to see if they will work. It's a continuous cycle that you can do over and over until you find the perfect steps and coping mechanisms for that particular fear.

When you are able to conquer your least fear, you can proceed with your other fears, until you're able to manage all of your fears. So start from the fear that has the least magnitude and end with the fear that has the highest magnitude of threat.

Chapter 9: Work Sheets for Fear and Anxiety Management

Here are the work sheets again; you can pick those that are applicable to your activity.

Date	Fear	Steps to implement	Coping Mechanisms	Evaluation

Type of Fear

Steps to implement

Coping mechanism

Evaluation

Notes

Date	Feared Situations	Anxiety rating (before) 0-10	Anxiety rating (during) 0-10	Anxiety rating (after) 0-10	Length of time in min.	Previous Thoughts	Reactions Comment Observations (after)

Chapter 10: Recording Your Thought Processes

It helps to record all your thought processes regarding your fears and anxieties so that you will know where you stand. You can record them before, during or after each activity. There are no fast rules, you can record them too anytime you feel it's necessary.

Nevertheless, this activity is most useful when you're trying to find coping strategies for your fears.

Since, we're trying to change your negative thoughts into positive thoughts, you can use your logbook to write them down.

At the onset of your activities, you may write whatever thoughts that come to your mind, even if they are negative, and then opposite the negative thought, write down its positive counterpart.

Concentrate on that positive counterpart and psyche yourself every morning and evening, focusing on them. Refer to chapter 4.

Example

Table 11

Situations	Thoughts	If negative, give opposite thoughts	Emotions	Behaviors
Speaking in front of a group	I might become tongue-	I will speak smoothly	>scared >anxious	>trembling fingers >can't keep

	tied			still

Change the negative thoughts into positive ones, every time you encounter them. Don't dwell on the negative thoughts. Always, switch to the positive thought whenever the negative thought starts to come in.

As your mind becomes accustomed to the positive thoughts, your actions will eventually change, as well.

You can also use this table

Table 12

Situations	Thoughts (What I thought)	Emotions (What I felt)	Actions (What I did)	Unhelpful thoughts	What's the best response

Based on this table, you can analyze the event correctly and identify what was wrong. Next time the same incident happens, you can now modify your actions to a more positive response.

Don't forget to accomplish the table each time you encounter your fears. Do this until your thoughts, actions and emotions match the last column in the table – "what's the best response?" Obviously, you will get rid of the unhelpful thoughts to perform the best response.

Reframing

You can also reframe how you perceive things, people and event. Frame these things in a positive light in your mind, and your actions and behavior will improve.

Practice this:

- ➢ Search for the positive aspects first in any given situation.
- ➢ Focus on that positive aspect.
- ➢ Be thankful for what you have.
- ➢ Learn how to appreciate things around you.

Example

You were invited to a friend's birthday party. As soon as you entered the room, you had already a negative impression forming in your mind. That was how you process your thoughts previously – you find something negative. This time, change the way you think.

Look around you and search for all the positive things that you can observe: the lights are colorful; the people are having a good time; the house decors are nicely placed; the host is beautiful; the food is served generously; and other positive things in that party.

There are still many other positive things, if you look for them. No matter how grim the situation is, there will always be something positive, and that's what you should search for. Concentrate on the positive happenings of the day, as well.

Make reframing a habit in your life, and rest assured, you will eventually be able to eliminate your automatic negative thoughts to automatic positive thoughts. This will change your behavior to a positive one.

It can be difficult, but you have to keep trying if you want to manage your fears, anxieties, anger and depression once and for all.

You can use the table in this chapter together with the Tables 1 to 10 to achieve the goals you have set for yourself.

Chapter 11: Evaluating Your Progress

This is an important phase of your CBT therapy. You must know how to evaluate your progress so that you can determine whether to proceed or not.

How can you evaluate your progress? You can do this by referring to your goals, and start from there.

Again, let's recall your main goal in using CBT. It is to change the way you think to change the way you feel, act, and behave. Since you are inclined to think negatively because of your psychological disorder, CBT will help convert you into an optimist, a person who thinks positively.

In the previous chapters, steps and strategies are presented to help you acquire the habit of thinking positively.

Now, let's evaluate your progress. You have to do this homework every day.

Table 13

Date	Feared Situations	Anxiety rating (before) 0-10	Anxiety rating (during) 0-10	Anxiety rating (after) 0-10	Length of time in min.	Previous Thoughts	Reactions Comment Observations (after)

Accomplish this homework while going through your daily activities. The column, 'Feared Situations' are your specific fears, what fears did you encounter during the day? Rate the anxiety caused by these fears, before, during and after the situation.

Note the length of time in minutes that your anxiety remained. For "Previous Thoughts" write down what you thought before the incident. Write down everything, whether they are negative or positive thoughts. What would happen? What's the worst scenario? What's the probability that your fear would happen?

On the column "Reaction, Comments, Observations, write down the actions you did, how your anxiety was affected, what helped you overcome the anxiety and what didn't help. You must also jot down what you would not do next time the same situation happens.

Write all your observations in the table. This would serve as a guide when similar situations occur again.

After you have completed your homework, evaluate your table and determine if there are any improvements, as you continue to be in the same situation throughout the week.

If the one-week data is not enough, you can extend the activity until you have acquired the habit of thinking positively, and until your mind can affect positively how you feel and behave.

The CBT treatment is short but effective. If you're visiting a psychologist or a psychotherapist, usually, it may take 10 to 20 sessions only, 1 hour per session for 3 to 6 months. The length of therapy will depend on how severe your psychological problems are. It's quite expensive, as well.

The large chunk of the job is for you to do your homework and practice every day. You should practice until you can gain control of your life and be psychologically healthy.

Your automatic negative thoughts and dysfunctional assumptions should be gradually channeled to more positive thoughts as you repeat the cycle every day.

Keeping a thought journal is important to determine your progress and assess if you're going anywhere.

Chapter 12: Understanding Your Anger and Depression

Your anger and depression can be managed properly, just like your fear and anxiety, if you use appropriate techniques.

The first thing that you should remember is that anger is a natural emotion that humans often feel, so it's normal. But this anger should be within the bounds of sanity.

That's why you have your reasoning power so you could think properly. A sane and civilized person doesn't burst in anger in public. He would manage his anger appropriately.

On the other hand, depression can be a result of mismanaged anger, extreme fear and anxiety. It could also result from the inability to cope with emotions and feelings. Depression can be debilitating and destructive.

If you're unable to manage your anger, and you feel depressed most of the time, it's high time you grab the steering wheel of your life and do away with all these pieces of negative baggage that you carry everywhere. They tend to slow you down and burden you. Do you want to go through life feeling that way?

Presumably the answer is no. Why else would you be reading this book?

Let's understand why you feel anger.

Anger is an expression of your emotion. It's normal to get angry when you're wronged or mistreated. But you must not allow your anger to take hold of your body. You're the master of your emotions and not the other way around.

Perceive anger as an emotion that you can control. If you know how to control it, you will be leading a happy life.

As for depression, the thoughts that may occur in your mind are negative:

- ➢ You blame yourself for everything that went wrong.
- ➢ You think you're nothing and worthless
- ➢ You feel that the world is hopeless

Then the physical symptoms of depression may emanate from your body. You will feel exhausted, you can't sleep, you can't eat, and your health deteriorates.

You don't have illnesses but because of your mind, you can get ill. That's how powerful your mind is.

By changing the way you think, you can escape from depression. You don't need to experience it. Depression can be 'cured' using the power of your thoughts.

As for anger, you can also learn how to control it. Anger is normal when you feel wronged, but you don't need to let the emotion rule you. You can learn the skills of managing your anger. You just have to be patient to learn it.

Chapter 13: Setting Your Goals to Cope with Anger and Depression

Before learning how to cope with your anger and depression, you have to set your goals first. What do you want to achieve? Be specific and clear about your goals.

You can pattern your goals with that of the goals that you have created in coping with your fears. Read in chapter 6 how you can create SMART goals.

Example

At the end of 1 month, I would be able to:

- Avoid angry outbursts in public
- Move away from the person who made me angry
- Avoid speaking, while still angry

At the end of 2 month, I would be able to:

- Avoid angry outbursts in public and at home
- Control my anger without leaving
- Speak in a calm voice in front of the person who caused the anger

Breaking your goals into small chunks will make the goal appear easier to achieve.

You could also create your long-term goals:

At the end of the CBT, I would be able to:

- Manage my anger in all situations

- Perform fruitful activities despite my anger
- Behave rationally in private and in public

Since depression comes as a result of your emotions, the goals that you have established, to control your fears and anger, can also encompass the goals you have for your depression.

If you fulfill your goals in coping with your fears and anger, your depression will be eliminated or controlled, as well.

Your ultimate goal is to stay positive amidst your anger and depression, so you can have complete control of your life. You can refer to the previous chapters for more information on preparing your goals.

Chapter 14: Implementing Your Goals to Cope with Anger and Depression

You're now set to implement your goals. In the same manner that you have coped with your fears and anxiety, you should also manage your anger and depression using the same methods.

All you have to do is to change "fear' into "anger" and change the entries to refer to anger and you're all set.

Step #1 – Identify situations that make you angry

Identify the events or situations that made you angry. In the logbook, prepare a new table and write all of them down. You should specify which situation caused you to be angry. You can include the intensity of the anger from a scale of 0 to 10.

Step #2 – Identify the steps you need to implement to curb your anger

For each of the situations, identify the steps you need to implement to be able to control your anger. Identify the specific steps should you perform to do this Prepare steps for each of the identified cause of anger.

Step #3 – Identify effective coping mechanisms for your anger

Identify the coping mechanisms or strategies that can be effective in controlling your anger. (Refer to previous chapter).

Step #4 - Evaluate the results.

Evaluating the results after implementing the coping mechanisms is an important step in coping with your anger. Was there a change in the manner that you had coped with your anger? Identify the coping mechanism that had worked effectively. What did not work? What would you do differently next time?

A sample table would look like this:

Table 14

Date	Cause of anger	Steps to implement	Coping Mechanisms	Evaluation
8/02	Rude person	>Step 1 – Learn how to perform breathing exercises. This must be done daily to achieve calm Step 2 - Meditate regularly Step 3 – Practice shutting up when angry. You can start with family members. Step 4 – Learn how to control your anger & how to keep calm in front of an angry person. You can practice with family	>Deep breaths to calm nerves during the heat of anger >Leaving the scene and going to some quiet place >writing down the cause of the anger >doing something productive to channel angry energy	>coping mechanism of deep breathing and leaving were effective

		members.		

As you work in managing your anger, you can learn more coping mechanisms that are effective for you. Don't be afraid to explore and experiment.

You can modify the worksheets used for fear and anxiety and use them for anger and depression.

Remember that the hard work of controlling your anger lies on you. It takes constant practice to succeed.

Likewise with depression, you can follow the steps in coping with your anger when dealing with your depression.

Practice, practice and practice because practice makes perfect.

Chapter 15: Recording Your Thought Processes

This process is the same with that of managing your fears. You can utilize the same form to monitor your progress. Only, this time, you're coping with your anger and depression.

Use any of the tables presented in chapter 8

Table 15

Situations (anger)	Thoughts	If negative, give opposite thoughts	Emotions	Behaviors
The woman was rude to me and I got angry	>I wanted to hit her >I wanted to lash back at her	>I'm not a thug. I won't hit her >I'm educated. I won't lash back.	>angry	>restless >tense

You could also use this table for more details:

Table 16

Situations	Thoughts (What I thought)	Emotions (What I felt)	Actions (What I did)	Unhelpful thoughts	What's the best response?

75

Through these tables, you can become aware of your thought processes. Thus, you can pinpoint dysfunctional thoughts (unhelpful thoughts) immediately, and identify the best response to that particular situation.

You should be open-minded to accept new ideas and ways to respond to situations. If you accomplish this activity properly, you will come to know that there are automatic thoughts that come to your mind, which are not justified or functional.

Example

Table 17

Situations	Thoughts (What I thought)	Emotions (What I felt)	Actions (What I did)	Unhelpful thoughts	What's the best response?
Rude woman	I wanted to slap her	angry	I shouted at her	Thoughts of slapping	Breathe deeply ad remain calm

Learn how to convert your dysfunctional thoughts to functional ones by accomplishing these tables.

Keeping tab of your tables will help you monitor your progress easily. Thus, your logbook must always be in sight.

Chapter 16: Evaluating Your Progress

Evaluating your progress is critical to make CBT succeed. Proper and correct evaluation procedures are also significant.

You can accomplish this phase just like what you did in evaluating your fears. Use the same table, but modify it to suit anger and depression

Remember to write in the details of each column. This way, your progress can be monitored accurately.

Date	Situations	Depression rating (before) 0-10	Depression rating (during) 0-10	Depression rating (after) 0-10	Length of time in min.	Previous Thoughts (before)	Reactions Comment Observations (after)
	Rude woman	8	8	8	120	I wanted to slap her	>I was relieved I didn't slap her >Because I controlled my anger, I didn't do anything unlawful

77

Every time you get into a situation similar to the one above, your behavior should have improved. Accomplish this table every time you encounter anger and depression to determine how your thought processes occur. The table will also show if your thoughts and behavior are becoming more positive.

The conversion of your negative thoughts to positive thoughts is the primary goal of all these activities. Therefore, evaluate your thoughts constantly, so you would not go astray from your goals.

Chapter 17: Mindfulness and Self-Reflection in CBT

Mindfulness Meditation and self-reflection can help you forge through your depression, fears and other psychological issues. Mindfulness Meditation is preferred than other types of meditation because it can serve as a self-reflection, simultaneously.

This is where the Mindfulness-Based Cognitive Therapy (MBCT) originated from. The combination of CBT and Mindfulness Meditation has provided excellent results in clinical studies in patients with insomnia, as well.

In chapter 4, the importance of knowing thyself and meditating were mentioned in passing. In this chapter, you will learn how to meditate using the Mindfulness Meditation method. Naturally, any type of meditation would do because all meditations can calm and appease the mind and body.

However, Mindfulness Meditation allows you to entertain your present thoughts, while most of the other meditations want you to empty your mind. Take note that the purpose of meditation in CBT is to manage and cultivate positive thoughts and do away with feelings of anxiety and depression to obtain peace and calm.

Here are the simple steps you can do:

Step #1 – Find a safe and secure place

This must be a private place where people cannot interrupt you. You may want to dim the lights. The place must not be too cold or too warm to make you uncomfortable. Set the best temperature that would make you comfortable.

You can listen to soft music if it helps you to concentrate, otherwise, turn it off.

Step #2 – Sit comfortably on a chair

Supine position can do too, but you may fall asleep. So, sitting down is recommended. Your back should be straight and the blade of your shoulders must be in line with your pubis.

If it's more convenient for you, you may want to assume the yoga Lotus position as explained in chapter 4.

If not, it's okay to sit on a chair. Just make sure, you're comfortable.

Step #3 – Start breathing in and out

Close your eyes and start your breathing exercises, so you can stabilize your mind and body. Breathe in deeply through your nose. Notice how the air rushes into your nose as you inhale the air.

Breathe out slowly using your mouth, creating a "ha" sound. Notice how the air leaves your body. While breathing in and out, mentally command your body to relax. Perform these several times until you establish a rhythm.

Step #4 – Be mindful of whatever emotions you feel at the moment

Relish the "now". Feel the sensations that come to your mind. If you're finding it difficult to absorb all the feelings and thoughts simultaneously, you may want to concentrate on one feeling.

Let's say your arms are giving you the sensation of warmth. Concentrate on the arms and savor that positive feeling. Think of positive thoughts. If a negative thought enters your mind, shoo it away and focus back on the positive thought, while being aware of the present.

Mindfulness will help you concentrate on your positive feelings, so that you can anchor on to them. These positive feelings will eventually replace your automatic negative thoughts.

With practice, you will know how to respond to negative emotions, and to find positive emotions to replace them.

Step #5 – Maintain your meditation for as long as possible

You can meditate for as long as you want. Your body should be relaxed. If it grows tense because of a negative thought that came to mind. Mentally instruct your muscles to relax, and then go back to thinking positive thoughts.

Examples of positive thoughts

- I'm relaxed.
- I'm happy.
- I'm healthy.
- I'm self-confident.
- I like spiders.
- I like wide spaces.
- I like to walk on side roads.

You may also want to instruct your muscles to relax in a more detailed manner. You can start with your feet, and then slowly go upwards to your head. Simply command silently that body portion to relax, as you breathe in and out.

That portion of your body can feel 'heavy' as the muscles switch to a 'resting' mode. When this happens, you can proceed to the next body part (feet, thighs, abdomen, chest, back, shoulders, arms, neck and then head).

This will enhance your ability to feel positive emotions. After the meditation, you will feel relaxed and happy, as well.

Step #6 – 'Wake up' from your meditation

Awaken your sleeping muscles and open your eyes. You can stand up to do a few stretches. Exercising after the meditation can be good for your health.

Conclusion

It has been proven that individuals who have undergone MBCT had fewer relapses. They also had quicker responses to therapy.

Clinical studies also showed that mindfulness has the ability to change the brain. In addition, paying attention to the present moment had increased the activation of the person's brain that deals with sadness and depression.

The brain's present-moment pathway is activated and this makes it easier for the person to deal with his negative emotions.

More and more experts are discovering the fact that meditation coupled with other modes of treatment is more effective.

Meditation doesn't only relax you but cures you, as well.

Chapter 18: Appraising Threats Accurately

For CBT to work effectively, you have to know how to appraise threats accurately. How can you do this? Here are steps that can help you do the task.

Create a table in your logbook and do the following steps:

Step #1 – Write down the threat

On the first column, write down the threats. You have to deal with them one-at-a-time. If you feel it a threat to you, it must be included in the list. Start from the situation that threatens you least, and deal with these threats based on their magnitude, until you reach the situation that threatens you the most.

Step #2 – Write down the worst thing that could happen to you

On the next column, write down what would be the worst thing that could happen to you. Include also predicted outcomes. Think of every possible scenario.

Step #3 – Write down what actually happened

In the third column, write down what actually happened. Include your own observations. Be specific. Write down the details carefully. Were your shoes untied? How did you walk to the stage? Did you make a beeline? Did you falter in your steps?

Step #4 – Evaluate if the threat you have feared most had actually happened

Did the thing you feared most happen? Write the details of what happened. You can also ask your family and friends, if they had felt the same threat and what happened afterwards.

Step #5 – Determine if the threat is real

Based on your evaluation in step #4, determine if the threat was real. Did the threat result to the fearful incident that you have predicted? If not, then the threat is not real. You have to change your automatic thought to the correct thought.

Your table will look this way:

Perceived threat	Worst scenario	What actually happened	Evaluate (did the scenario happen?)	Is the threat real?

You have to describe the details of the worst scenario, so that a clear picture of the situation can be evaluated reliably.

When to seek the help of a psychotherapist

Apply the techniques in this book for 6 months. If there are no changes in your behavior, there may be an underlying disease that interferes with the therapy. Visit your doctor and request some diagnostic laboratory tests to determine what's wrong with your body.

If there's nothing wrong with your body, you can visit a psychotherapist, a psychiatrist, or a psychologist. You may have a severe mental illness that has to be treated with medications.

But, think positively. You may merely need a few more months to make things work. Not all persons learn alike.

Chapter 19: How You Can Take Back Control of Your Life

You can only take back control of your life, if you are determined to do so. Recognizing your will power to do this challenging endeavor is the first crucial step. Only you can be the master of your mind and body.

As explained in the previous chapters, you have to change the way you think, so you could get free from your psychological disorders. Thinking positively is the main key of freeing yourself from the shackles of your dysfunctional mind.

Vital strategies on how to do this are already presented in the previous chapters. Go over them and apply them. Application is significant for the change in your mind-set to occur.

Thus, you can only control your life if you practice to control it. Constant practice will eventually allow you to do so. It's like learning how to drive; you have to practice driving to learn the skill.

So, don't be 'lazy' to accomplish the homework assigned every day. You have to be patient in recording your thoughts, processing and evaluating them. To summarize what you should do, read below:

1. Recognize the power of your mind.

2. Set your goals by writing down what you want to accomplish in relation to your fears.

3. Realize that your fears are based on how you perceive situations.

4. Determine if your fears are dysfunctional or not. If they are, do away with them.

5. Reframe your mind to focus only on positive thoughts.

6. Continue your thought journal and monitor your entries, so you can reframe promptly when your thoughts turn negative.

7. Do away with your distorted view of things every second of your life.

8. When your thought is dysfunctional accept your mistake, and adjust your thoughts accordingly.

9. Let your thoughts control your behavior positively.

10. Observe what you learned from CBT every day and you will have taken back control of your life.

If you have not taken back control of your life after you have done this, then you may have an underlying condition that should be treated with medications. You have to consult your doctor.

Sometimes, it may take a longer time for you to inculcate optimism in your life.

Therefore, be patient and wait a little longer.

Chapter 20: Valuable Tips in Cognitive Behavioral Therapy

CBT is broad and it involves many disciplines, but the useful topics related to how you can take back control of your life are found in this book. There are more essential facts that you could learn from CBT for these tips. These valuable tips can act as guidelines in your quest to control your life.

1. **Always be positive.** This should be your by-word. You don't have time to be negative because if you do, all your work and hardships would be for naught. CBT is optimism.

2. **Do your homework religiously.** This is how you can learn your skills, and this is how you can conquer your fears. Accomplish your homework daily. As you do it, you're also practicing it. Think of it as your 'eternal' homework. Learn to love it.

3. **Relapse can happen.** Thus, you have to continue accomplishing your tables. You don't only learn how to cope with your fear and anger, your personality will also change for the better.

4. **Practice noticing negative automatic behaviors.** This will help you prevent negative thoughts from entering your mind. Your mind causes your behaviors. If you think negatively, you will act negatively. Thus, practice throwing away the negative thoughts at the onset.

5. **CBT can be difficult at first.** However, as you practice and grow accustomed to the process, you will be more comfortable. Also, there may be no visible changes in your personality for months. But, if you

persist, you will be transformed gradually into that beautiful person that you are.

6. **CBT is not for everyone.** Persons with serious psychological disorders may need medication and psychiatric treatment. Hence, if it doesn't work for you after several months, you have to seek treatment elsewhere.

7. **Cognitive skills are important**. You should develop cognitive skills, such as reframing, positive thinking, and similar activities for CBT to be successful. Hone your cognitive skills so you can do CBT properly.

8. **Reading more self-help materials is encouraged.** You should read more self-help materials. These materials can aid you in your endeavor. With online apps available, you can browse online to achieve your goal. There are also interactive online computer interfaces for CBT that you can explore.

9. **CBT can prevent the worsening of the condition of anxiety-ridden patient**s. Some experts had found out that anxiety-ridden patients have slowly recovered from their illnesses. CBT had helped cure their anxiety disorders. This is a fact that experts acknowledge. Have faith and do your homework.

10. **You can draw moral support from your family.** If you feel you need moral support, you can ask your family and friends to assist you in your quest. Receiving a pat on the back and a warm hug can do wonders to your morale.

11. **Computerized CBT or CCBT can treat depression and anxiety**. This is an update for CBT. Apparently, it's as useful as non-computerized CBT.

Nonetheless, the person-to-person encounter is still the best.

12. **Don't give up easily**. Move forward with determination even when things are not going your way. There may be times that you will feel discouraged during the therapy because no one is supporting you, and you aren't getting any better. This is the time that you need CBT the most. Now, apply what you have learned in this particular situation.

13. **Self-awareness is a vital part of CBT**. If you're not aware of yourself, you will not succeed in CBT. This is so because CBT is about knowing your own thoughts, feelings, actions and behavior.

14. **Recording is essential to CBT**. If you don't record or write down your thoughts, it would be difficult to monitor your progress, and to evaluate your results. When you have something to record, it also indicates that you have practiced CBT.

15. **After a job well done, congratulate yourself.** You have succeeded in your goal because of your diligence and dedication. CBT can never triumph, unless you have done your task well. Congratulations!

These are some of the tips that you must remember. Refer to these guidelines whenever you need them. If you play it right, CBT can change your life forever. Grab this chance to change your life for the better.

Conclusion

CBT is an alternative treatment for psychological disorders that you could utilize to get your life back. You can eliminate and manage those fears, anxieties and depression effectively if you comply with the CBT techniques presented in this book.

Don't be afraid to explore and modify the methods to fit your needs. In addition, remember to do your assignment every day to learn the skills. Skills can be learned and not inherited, so don't be discouraged when you can't do it at first. Keep trying and everything will fall back into place.

Have faith in yourself and in your abilities. You have succeeded in taking control of your life.

Good luck with your CBT journey. Think positive, act positive. Your life is now back in your hands. Live it successfully.

www.ingramcontent.com/pod-product-compliance
Lightning Source LLC
Chambersburg PA
CBHW070312230526
45470CB00002B/841